Illegal Aliens

Illegal Aliens:
Problems and Policies

American Enterprise Institute for Public Policy Research
Washington, D.C.

ISBN 0-8447-0214-5
Legislative Analysis No. 32, 95th Congress
October 18, 1978
Price $2.00 per copy

CONTENTS

INTRODUCTION

An illegal alien is a foreign national who has entered the United States sur-
reptitiously or by fraud or has violated the terms of lawful entry by, for
example, overstaying a tourist visa or accepting unauthorized employment.
As shown in Table 1, the United States has historically welcomed immigrants
—more than 47 million people since 1820. Table 1 also indicates, at least in
part, the extent of the problem addressed by the current legislation: the huge
number of illegal aliens in this country.

Almost 10 million illegal aliens have been apprehended by the Immigration
and Naturalization Service (INS) of the U.S. Department of Justice since
1920. But though the apprehension rate has risen, according to INS Commissioner Leonard Chapman INS is catching only one out of ten.[1] For
obvious reasons, the total number of illegal aliens currently in the United
States is not known. The problem is illustrated by the following citation from
a study of immigration policy by Elliott Abrams and Franklin S. Abrams:

> A House subcommittee estimated the number [of illegal aliens] at
> between one and two million, and the INS Commissioner, former
> Marine Corps Commandant General Leonard Chapman, recently
> told Congress the total is four or five million. The unreliability of
> the figure was demonstrated when Chapman was asked how he
> arrived at it: "It is just a midpoint between two extremes. I have
> heard one or two million at one end of the scale and eight or ten
> million at the other. So, I am selecting a midpoint . . . just a guess,
> that is all. Nobody knows." Each year hundreds of thousands of
> deportable aliens are located, [but] extrapolation from those statis-
> tics is clearly unreliable, since, as Chairman Rodino (D-N.J.) noted
> at the 1971 House hearings on illegal immigration, "The number of
> apprehensions of aliens illegally in the United States appears to be
> in direct proportion to the number of Immigration and Naturaliza-
> tion Service officers who are available."[2]

The variation in the number of apprehensions with the level of effort expended
is apparent in Table 1. During the 1950s a concerted effort was made through
Operation Wetback to locate Mexican illegals, and in 1954 alone more than
a million illegal aliens were expelled. Because much of the manpower and
resources of the INS is concentrated in the Southwest along the Mexican border, the majority of illegal aliens apprehended are Mexicans, as reported in
Table 2. This allocation of manpower and resources also reflects the fact

1

Table 1

Immigration to the United States and Illegal Aliens Apprehended, by Decade, 1821–1970, and by Year, 1971–1975

Period	Number of Immigrants	Illegal Aliens Apprehended
1821–1830	143,439	
1831–1840	599,125	
1841–1850	1,713,251	
1851–1860	2,598,214	
1861–1870	2,314,824	
1871–1880	2,812,191	
1881–1890	5,246,613	
1891–1900	3,687,564	
1901–1910	8,795,386	
1911–1920	5,735,811	
1921–1930	4,107,209	128,484 [a]
1931–1940	528,431	147,457
1941–1950	1,035,039	1,377,210
1951–1960	2,515,479	3,584,229
1961–1970	3,321,677	1,608,356
1971	370,478	420,126
1972	384,685	505,949
1973	400,063	655,968
1974	394,861	788,145
1975	386,194	766,600

[a] First recorded in 1925.

Source: U.S. Department of Justice, Immigration and Naturalization Service, *1975 Annual Report*, pp. 31 and 90.

that the Mexican-U.S. border is the single largest entry area for illegal aliens. Illegal aliens come to the United States from most countries of the world, however, and are found throughout the nation, although they tend to concentrate in cities.

Table 2

Illegal Aliens Apprehended, by Fiscal Year, 1966–1975

Year	Total Apprehended	Mexicans Apprehended	Mexicans as a Percentage of Total
1966	138,520	89,751	65
1967	161,608	108,327	67
1968	212,057	151,705	72
1969	283,557	201,636	71
1970	345,353	277,377	80
1971	420,126	348,178	83
1972	505,949	430,213	85
1973	655,968	576,823	88
1974	788,145	709,959	90
1975	766,600	680,392	89

Source: U.S. Congress, Committee on the Judiciary, *Illegal Aliens: Analysis and Background*, 1977, p. 5.

The purpose of this analysis is to provide an overview of the issues related to illegal aliens in the United States and to discuss the arguments for and against the legislation currently pending before the Congress. The analysis contains a brief legislative history, which focuses primarily on immigration legislation since 1952, and presents background material on the economic and social impacts of illegal aliens in the United States. Also included is a brief discussion of alternative proposals.

LEGISLATIVE HISTORY AND BACKGROUND

With the exception of the Alien Act of 1798, which permitted the president to expel "dangerous" aliens, no constraints were placed on immigration until qualitative restrictions were imposed in the 1880s, when convicts, prostitutes, lunatics, and idiots were barred. The first legislation dealing specifically with illegal aliens was an 1888 amendment to the contract labor laws, which called for the deportation of aliens entering the country in violation of the laws.[3]

The Immigration Act of 1917[4] was the first systematic arrangement of the existing statutes on immigration. This act introduced a literacy requirement for immigrants along with restrictions on Orientals. Quotas were first assigned in the Immigration Act of 1924,[5] which restricted immigration from Eastern Hemisphere countries to a proportion of the number of persons, of specified national origin, in the United States at the time of the 1920 census. In addition, no more than 150,000 immigrants a year could be admitted from the Eastern Hemisphere. Immigration from the Western Hemisphere remained unrestricted.

The McCarran-Walter Act (Immigration and Nationality Act of 1952)[6] superseded all previous immigration legislation. It continued the quota system for Eastern Hemisphere immigrants and unrestricted immigration for Western Hemisphere immigrants. This act is still the basic law governing immigration in the United States, but significant changes have been made over the years. The Immigration and Nationality Act Amendments of 1965 abolished the old quota system and replaced it with an annual ceiling of 170,000 on immigrants from Eastern Hemisphere countries and a corresponding limit of 120,000 on Western Hemisphere countries.[7] It was the first time restrictions of this type had been imposed on this hemisphere. Eastern Hemisphere immigration was further restricted to 20,000 immigrants per country per year, selected through a preference system in which each of seven categories is limited to a certain proportion of the visas available. The categories are: (1) unmarried sons and daughters, over twenty-one years of age, of U.S. citizens; (2) spouses and unmarried children of aliens lawfully admitted for permanent residence; (3) members of the professions and scientists and artists of exceptional ability; (4) married sons and daughters of U.S. citizens; (5) brothers and sisters of U.S. citizens; (6) skilled and unskilled workers needed in the United States; and (7) refugees. The Immigration and Nationality Act Amendments of

1976[8] merely extended to the Western Hemisphere the 20,000 per country limit and the preference system.

The Immigration and Nationality Act of 1952, as amended, contains several sections directly applicable to illegal aliens. Section 275 (8 U.S.C. 1325) deals specifically with criminal sanctions for illegal aliens. If an alien enters the United States without inspection by the INS or is admitted as a result of misrepresentation or fraud, he or she is guilty of a misdemeanor, punishable by up to six months' imprisonment or a $500 fine or both. Second and subsequent offenses are felonies, punishable by not more than two years' imprisonment or a $1,000 fine or both.

Section 274 (8 U.S.C. 1324) establishes criminal sanctions for individuals organizing or aiding the illegal entry of aliens. Smuggling, harboring, transporting, or encouraging illegal aliens is a felony offense punishable by imprisonment for up to five years or a fine of up to $2,000 or both for each alien involved. The employment of illegal aliens, by itself, is not an illegal act, and employers of illegal aliens are specifically exempt from prosecution.

Finally, according to section 245(c) (8 U.S.C. 1255 [c]), aliens who violate their terms of entry by accepting employment cannot change their status from nonimmigrant to permanent resident alien (immigrant) so long as they remain in this country.

Other legislation pertaining to illegal aliens includes the 1974 amendments to the Farm Labor Contractor Registration Act of 1963,[9] which provides a criminal penalty of three years' imprisonment or a fine of up to $10,000 or both for contractors not registered under the act who intentionally hire illegal aliens. The Social Security Act Amendments of 1972[10] specify that social security numbers may be issued only to those aliens entitled to work in the United States and those applying for or receiving benefits under federal welfare programs. Alien applicants for social security numbers must produce proof of their entitlement or face a criminal penalty of up to one year's imprisonment or a fine of up to $1,000 or both. To be eligible for public assistance programs the alien must have been lawfully admitted as an immigrant or must be permanently residing in the United States under color of law. The 1976 Unemployment Compensation Amendments to the Internal Revenue Code[11] restrict unemployment compensation to immigrant aliens.

The economic and social impact of illegal aliens in the United States—the demands they place on social services and the nature of their involvement in the nation's labor markets—depends on the total number in the population, their geographical distribution, and their personal characteristics (age, level of education, and number of dependents). Although data on the total number are not reliable, studies of a sample of apprehended illegal aliens provide some indication of their personal characteristics.

6

A recent survey prepared by David S. North and Marion S. Houstoun contains useful detail and breaks down responses by region of origin (Mexico, Western Hemisphere, and Eastern Hemisphere).[12] On the basis of their sample of 793 apprehended illegal aliens, sixteen years of age or more, who had worked for wages at least two weeks in the United States, North and Houstoun describe the typical illegal alien as:

- a young adult (78.1 percent of the sample was thirty-four years old or less)

- a male (90.8 percent of the sample)

- economically motivated (74.2 percent come to the United States to get a job)

- supporting at least one relative or dependent in the country of origin (79.7 percent)

- relatively unskilled and uneducated with roughly half as much education as his counterpart in the U.S. labor force (6.7 years as against 12.4 years of schooling)

- less likely to be married than his U.S. counterpart

- unable to speak English (63.9 percent of respondents).[13]

The subjects of the North and Houstoun study group were not homogeneous; personal characteristics differed considerably, depending on the region of origin. Even with these differences, it is reasonable to conclude that, in comparison with the U.S. norm, the illegal alien appears to be an economically motivated, disadvantaged young adult male.

Labor Market Impacts

Given the economic motivation of illegal aliens in coming to the United States and their personal characteristics, it is not surprising that they actively compete with U.S. workers in the secondary job market for low-wage, low-skill, and low-status jobs. Table 3 compares the employment of illegal aliens in the United States with their occupations in their country of origin. About 63 percent of the respondents from Mexico had been employed as laborers or service workers when in Mexico, but only 10 percent of the Eastern Hemisphere respondents had worked in these occupations in their home countries. Regardless of region of origin, illegal aliens employed in professional and managerial work in their home countries were very likely to move down the employment scale to less-skilled jobs in the United States. In contrast, those workers at the lowest end of the skill scale in their country of origin often were able to move up the economic ladder by coming to the United States.

Table 3

**Occupation of Apprehended Illegal Alien Respondents in their
Country of Origin and in Most Recent U.S. Job, by Region of Origin**

(as percentage of group responding)

Occupational Group	Total		Mexican Illegals		Western Hemisphere Illegals		Eastern Hemisphere Illegals	
	Country of origin	U.S.	Country of origin	U.S.	Country of origin	U.S.	Country of origin	U.S.
Professional and technical workers	5.6	1.6	1.7	0.5	10.4	1.7	20.8	10.4
Owners, managers, administrators (nonfarm)	2.9	1.3	0.2	—	6.4	1.7	12.5	10.4
Sales workers	5.3	1.1	3.2	0.7	9.8	1.2	6.3	4.2
Clerical workers	3.8	1.4	1.7	—	7.5	4.1	8.3	4.2
Craftspersons	14.8	15.3	15.0	14.3	15.0	13.3	12.5	31.2
Machine operators	13.5	24.5	8.4	21.9	22.0	36.4	27.1	4.2
Transport drivers	4.1	0.6	4.4	0.7	4.6	0.6	—	—
Nonfarm laborers	9.1	14.8	11.8	17.9	4.6	11.6	2.1	—
Farmers	0.3	—	0.2	—	0.6	—	—	—
Farm laborers	35.4	18.8	49.1	27.0	12.1	4.6	2.1	—
Service workers, except private household	3.3	17.4	2.2	13.5	5.2	21.4	6.3	35.4
Private household workers	1.9	3.2	2.0	3.4	1.7	3.5	2.1	—
Number of Respondents	628	628	407	407	173	173	48	48

Dash (—): Negligible.
Source: North and Houstoun, "The Characteristics and Role of Illegal Aliens," p. 108.

According to North and Houstoun, "The U.S. labor market thus tended to homogenize what were otherwise distinctly heterogeneous groups of illegals." [14]

The impact of illegal aliens in the secondary labor market and the concomitant displacement of American workers supplies the major argument for advocates of legislation to restrict the employment of illegal aliens. They argue that the presence of illegal aliens tends to depress wages and to perpetuate poor working conditions. The data from the North and Houstoun study, reported in Table 4, seem to support this contention. As a group, illegal aliens are paid considerably less an hour than is the average U.S. laborer. Illegal aliens obtained only 35 percent of the average hourly wage paid to U.S. workers in the mining industry and 42 percent of the average in contract construction. Although in finance, real estate, and insurance the illegal aliens were paid 81 percent of the average hourly wage, overall they

8

Table 4

Average Gross Hourly and Weekly Wage, and Weekly Hours, of Apprehended Illegal Alien Respondents in their Most Recent U.S. Job and of U.S. Production or Nonsupervisory Workers (PNW), by Industry, in 1975

Industry	Average Hourly Wage (dollars)		Average Weekly Wage (dollars)		Average Weekly Hours		Number of Illegals[a]
	Illegals	U.S. PNW	Illegals	U.S. PNW	Illegals	U.S. PNW	
Agriculture, forestry, and fisheries	2.07	—[b]	110.57	—[b]	53.6	—[b]	134
Mining	2.00	5.79	120.00	244.92	60.0	42.3	1
Contract construction	2.98	7.15	126.39	265.27	42.8	37.1	124
Manufacturing	2.92	4.73	121.22	184.47	41.2	39.0	259
Transportation and public utilities	2.77	5.75	134.00	228.28	48.6	39.7	10
Trade: Wholesale and retail	2.57	3.71	112.69	124.66	43.4	33.6	152
Finance, real estate, and insurance	3.32	4.08	117.00	148.10	36.0	36.3	6
Services, except private household	2.79	3.98	121.75	134.13	45.0	33.7	57
Private household services	1.63	—[b]	66.30	—[b]	42.4	—[b]	23

[a] Twenty-seven illegals were self-employed or did not respond.

[b] North and Houstoun excluded from comparison with U.S. workers 134 illegals employed in agriculture and 23 in private household service.

Source: North and Houstoun, "The Characteristics and Role of Illegal Aliens," p. 125.

received only 60 percent of the average paid to U.S. production or nonsupervisory workers. Of 793 respondents, however, 455, or 57 percent, had been apprehended in either California, Texas, or Arizona, which weighted the study sample disproportionately toward the Southwest.[15] The place where the aliens were apprehended is apparently important in determining hourly rates of pay. Of 1,500 illegal aliens apprehended in Detroit from February through October

1976, INS reported that 900 held jobs, and the distribution of hourly wages was:

Percent of Total	Hourly Wage
31	$6.50 or more
39	$4.50–$6.50
22	$2.50–$4.50
9	$2.50 or less[16]

Because 70 percent of the working illegal aliens in the sample from Detroit made in excess of $4.50 per hour, it is reasonable to conclude that wage scales depend on the labor market in which the alien works. Rates of pay reported by North and Houstoun may be biased downward because their sample was heavily weighted toward the Southwest, where aliens from Mexico tend to cluster. It is, of course, unknown what level of wages would obtain in Detroit or the Southwest in the absence of illegal alien workers.

Evidence that wage rates in the labor market along the U.S.-Mexican border are not depressed significantly by illegal aliens has been presented in a study by Barton Smith and Robert Newman. They conclude that:

> The findings of this study indicate that nominal, real and expected real incomes (reflecting wage differences) are lower in the border area than the non-border region. After accounting for a variety of sociodemographic characteristics, the nominal income differential is approximately $1,680 or roughly 20 percent. Though this differential is significant, it is substantially smaller than differences produced from an examination of data published by the Bureau of Labor Statistics, commonly cited by activists and academicians alike. These results cast doubt on the validity of BLS average wage data for a variety of cross-section labor market analyses and emphasize the importance of controlling adequately for differences in labor characteristics before making even nominal wage comparisons.
>
> More important it was found that after controlling for variations in the cost of living between regions, annual real incomes are $684 less in the border area than in Houston, an approximate 8 percent differential. This clearly indicates that if migration from Mexico is having a negative impact on wages along the border it is not as severe as many have contended. In fact, this differential is of the order of magnitude that it could represent the implicit premium that individuals along the border are willing to pay for nonpecuniary advantages such as remaining close to their cultural heritage.[17]

It is clear from Table 4 that average weekly wages of the respondents in the North and Houstoun study are more comparable to those of U.S. workers than are their average hourly rates of pay. For example, on an hourly basis, the average illegal alien in the service industry receives only 70 percent as much as his U.S. counterpart; on a weekly basis, however, the same illegal alien receives 91 percent of the average wages of U.S. service workers. The rates of pay between illegals and U.S. workers are more comparable on a weekly than on an hourly basis because, as reported in Table 4, the illegal alien works more hours on the average than the U.S. worker. Smith and Newman were aware of the differences in income created by differences in hours worked. They state that "regional differences were also estimated using both income and average wages as the dependent variable. The empirical results of all three approaches were quite similar and the analysis and findings of border/non-border differentials were especially robust."[18] This statement indicates that the same conclusions apply whether hourly wage differentials or weekly income differentials are employed in their analysis.

Smith and Newman offer some interesting explanations for their finding that illegal aliens do not have as severe an impact on wages as is often believed:

> Several explanations might be given to explain the less than expected real income differential that exists; however, two seem most plausible. First, immigrants from Mexico may merely be taking unwanted jobs that resident labor avoids. Second, it may be that both Anglo-American and Mexican-American labor are highly mobile and that large scale internal migration to other work centers in the United States may prevent wage disparities from becoming too large.[19]

The first conclusion is of particular interest, for it is in direct opposition to "conventional wisdom." It is often argued by those who support more stringent legislation to control illegal aliens that aliens take jobs from U.S. citizens. Common sense supports the idea that every job held by an alien is one less job for a U.S. citizen and that the unemployment rate is, therefore, higher than it would be in the absence of illegal aliens in the labor market. *U.S. News and World Report* stated that "Ray Marshall, Secretary of Labor and an expert in illegal immigration, says that any effort to solve the unemployment problem in the U.S. must also deal with the illegal-alien problem."[20] *Business Week*, in a similar vein, suggested that "Because of illegal workers, the unemployment figures are significantly higher than they would otherwise be. It is impossible for the U.S. to provide jobs for the whole world's unemployed, but because it is the richest and freest of the large economies, the country is drawing them in increasing numbers."[21]

The U.S. Immigration and Naturalization Service, as reported in Table 5, has projected that a million jobs for Americans could be created by enforcing immigration policies. Nearly two-thirds of these potential jobs are in agriculture and the service industries. About 55 percent of the million potential jobs would be created in the Southwest.

11

Table 5
Projected Number of Jobs That Could Be Created by
Enforcing Immigration Policies
(thousands)

Location	Agri-culture	Heavy Industry	Light Industry	Service	Total
Northeast	1.00	35.00	58.00	72.00	166.00
Boston, Mass.	0.00	2.00	2.00	2.50	6.50
Hartford, Conn.	0.00	0.75	1.25	3.00	5.00
Newark, N.J.	0.00	5.00	14.00	6.00	25.00
New York, N.Y.	0.00	24.00	32.00	50.00	106.00
Other	1.00	3.25	8.75	10.50	23.50
Southeast	30.00	15.00	25.00	49.00	120.00
Miami, Fla.	13.00	6.00	12.00	21.00	52.00
San Juan, P.R.	0.00	1.50	3.50	8.00	13.00
Philadelphia, Pa.	0.00	2.00	3.00	4.00	9.00
Washington, D.C.	0.00	2.50	3.00	6.00	11.50
Other	17.00	3.00	4.50	10.00	34.50
Northwest	56.00	25.00	30.00	45.00	156.00
Chicago, Ill.	8.50	19.00	21.00	31.00	79.50
Detroit, Mich.	4.20	2.50	4.00	9.00	19.70
Kansas City, Mo.	2.00	1.50	1.50	2.00	7.00
Helena, Mont.	9.50	0.00	0.50	1.00	11.00
Havre, Mont.	15.00	0.00	0.00	0.00	15.00
Other	16.80	2.00	3.00	2.00	23.80
Southwest	248.00	75.00	100.00	135.00	558.00
Denver, Colo.	15.00	3.00	3.00	7.00	28.00
Livermore, Cal.	100.00	2.00	3.00	5.00	110.00
Los Angeles, Cal.	6.00	29.00	50.00	50.00	135.00
Dallas, Tex.	2.50	10.00	10.00	30.00	52.50
San Francisco, Cal.	1.50	1.00	2.00	2.00	6.50
Border cities	100.00	20.00	30.00	40.00	190.00
Other	23.00	10.00	2.00	1.00	36.00
Total U.S.	335.00	150.00	214.00	301.00	1,000.00

Source: U.S. Congress, House of Representatives, Committee on Government Operations, Subcommittee on Legal and Monetary Affairs, *Immigration and Naturalization Service Regional Office Operations,* 93d Cong., 2d sess., August 13, September 12, 17, and 18, and October 9, 1974, p. 579.

In contrast to the assertions of *U.S. News and World Report, Business Week,* and INS, some have argued that U.S. workers do not wish to fill jobs currently held by illegal aliens.

The U.S. Labor Department has increased its efforts to keep all foreigners out of the orchards. This year, according to Washington Attorney S. Steven Karalekas, who represents a group of apple growers from ten East Coast states, the growers had to appear before five district courts in five states, two U.S. courts of appeals and Supreme Court Justice William Brennan before they finally got approval to bring in foreign labor. The Federal Government has insisted that the orchard owners seek American workers, using imported labor only as a last resort. The growers argue that even past intensive recruiting programs in inner-city neighborhoods such as Harlem in New York City and Roxbury in Boston, as well as among the unemployed in Vermont, failed to attract nearly enough qualified pickers. In Harlem, a $10,000 recruitment drive mounted by the Department of Labor last year attracted only 75 job applicants. Only 15 reported to work—and all of them quit within a week. Says Grower Hermann: "I think it's become a case of harassment. The Labor people have the facts: there just aren't enough Americans willing and qualified to pick apples." Or as Bolton Orchard owner Robert Davis complains, "We know how to get the apples off. We just want the right to get them off."[22]

Thus, some have argued that there is not a surplus of American workers in the secondary labor markets but a shortage of labor, and illegal aliens are hired to fill the gaps. One proponent of this thesis is M.I.T. economist Michael J. Piore, who views the tremendous increase in illegal immigration into the United States over the past decade as an integral part of the socioeconomic development of an industrialized society:

> Adult native workers in any industrial society tend regularly to reject secondary jobs because of low social status and the instability and lack of career opportunity which they carry. These jobs, however, tend to carry much higher relative status in the social structures of rural agricultural communities. That and the fact that rural workers who migrate to urban areas generally expect to stay only temporarily and are therefore less interested in career opportunity and work stability make migrants an attractive source of labor for the secondary sector and they are recruited for that purpose.[23]

Migrant alien labor has been employed in the United States to relieve labor shortages in the past. In 1942 a treaty was negotiated between the United States and Mexico which allowed Mexican farm workers entry on a temporary basis to relieve the manpower shortages caused by World War II. This treaty was the basis for the Bracero Program, which survived for twenty-two years (until December 31, 1964) and involved about 4.8 million Mexican workers. It has been asserted that "Without question, its [the Bracero Program] existence and termination are causes of the current illegal alien program."[24]

Statements about a shortage of workers in the secondary labor market at the present time carry additional weight since the drop of the unemployment rate to about 6 percent. In 1962 the "full-employment" rate of unemployment was set at 4 percent by the Council of Economic Advisers in their Annual Report, and for years this rate has been regarded as the goal of public policy. In the 1977 Annual Report, however, the council stated that the full-employment rate of unemployment was now at least 4.9 percent and possibly as high as 5.5 percent. According to Phillip Cagan, the increase in the full-employment rate of unemployment is attributable to two factors: changes in the composition of the labor force—that is, "the proportion of people who move into and out of the labor force has grown"—and the expansion of government programs that encourage individuals to remain unemployed or discourage employers from hiring inexperienced workers.[25] Thus, some have questioned whether unemployment is as severe as commonly believed.

Impact on Taxes and Social Security

It is often argued that illegal aliens burden social programs such as those offering welfare, food stamps, and medical assistance and that taxpayers bear the expense. According to testimony before the Subcommittee on Immigration, Citizenship, and International Law of the House Judiciary Committee in September 1975:

> Federal, state and local governments, in general, have little information on the participation of illegal aliens in public assistance programs. This lack of precise data has made it impossible to accurately estimate the effects of illegal aliens on either a regional or national basis. It is evident, however, that the impact is substantial and increasingly state and local governments are turning to the federal government for reimbursement for services provided to illegal aliens.[26]

These conclusions were supported in a report by the General Accounting Office to the Senate Committee on the Budget, with the caveat that:

> Most studies are limited to local or regional areas, deal with only certain segments of the illegal alien population, and are based on assumptions unsupported by hard data. Where illegal aliens were interviewed, the possibility of untruthful answers exists. Where samples were taken, they were often too small to produce statistically sound results. This applies to our own studies and interviews.[27]

The GAO report summarized its findings and conclusions as follows:

> —Illegal aliens are collecting public assistance, but insufficient data exist to estimate the extent of use or financial impact on a nationwide basis.

> —Medical assistance, unemployment insurance, and public education may be the programs most used by illegal aliens.

> —Public assistance used by illegal aliens may place a greater financial burden on state and local government than on the Federal government.

—The indirect burden placed on public assistance programs by illegal aliens (such as displacing citizens in jobs, thus causing them to seek public assistance) may be greater than that caused by direct participation in the programs.

—Access to public assistance programs by illegal aliens can be obtained through (1) use of illicit documents, (2) absence of statutory or regulatory denial, (3) administrative error, or (4) court order.

—Illegal aliens contribute to our welfare system by paying taxes. Whether these payments are sufficient to offset benefits received is unknown.

—Public assistance benefit payments flowing from the United States to other countries do not appear to be significant.

—Public assistance programs do not appear to be a significant determinant of whether a person comes to or remains in the United States illegally.[28]

The GAO report categorizes as serious the problem of illicit documents, which are easily obtained, difficult to detect, and used by illegal aliens to qualify for various types of public assistance.[29]

Commissioner of Immigration Leonard Chapman stated, in 1976, that of 130 illegal aliens arrested in Yakima, Washington, "33 held food stamps to which they were not entitled, 17 more occupied low-cost government housing, and 16 were illegally on welfare."[30] He cited an independent study commissioned by INS which estimated that illegal aliens are milking U.S. taxpayers of $13 billion annually by taking jobs away from legal residents and forcing them into unemployment, by illegally taking welfare benefits, and by avoiding taxes.

Another, less well-known aspect of illegal aliens' effect on taxes centers on those who, while unlawfully residing in the United States, qualified to become legal residents. The qualifications necessary for immigrant status include marrying a U.S. citizen or permanent-resident alien, giving birth while in the United States (the child is a U.S. citizen), or obtaining work experience and job offers. The GAO report noted:

> These actions affect the public assistance system because many illegal aliens, after obtaining legal status, obtain public assistance . . . Large expenditures of tax monies—Federal and State—have been used in supporting immigrants and their families within five years after entry. For example, our analysis of 195 randomly selected immigrant welfare cases in Los Angeles County showed that 86 (44 percent) applied for assistance within five years after entering the United States. More than half of these applied within two years. Newly arrived immigrants and their families were re-

ceiving $19.6 million annually in welfare payments in Los Angeles County.[31]

From their survey, North and Houstoun provide some information (Table 6) on tax payments and the use of tax-supported public assistance programs by illegal aliens in their study.

More than three-fourths of North and Houstoun's respondents stated that social security payments were withheld, and almost as many reported the withholding of federal income taxes. Nearly half paid hospitalization insurance and about one-third filed federal income tax forms. Less than 2 percent obtained welfare payments, used food stamps, or were in job-training programs funded by the federal government. Less than 5 percent of the respondents reported having children in the U.S. schools or collecting one or more weeks of unemployment insurance, even though North and Houstoun reported an average unemployment rate of 10.2 percent on the part of the respondents.[32]

With regard to the role of illegal aliens as taxpayers, North and Houstoun conclude:

> Insofar as illegals are bona fide employees of bona fide employers, as a substantial percentage of the respondents were, they are making substantial tax contributions in the form of withholding taxes, in addition to whatever other tax contributions are automatic (e.g., sales taxes, which illegals pay in their role as consumer).[33]

But, as the GAO report pointed out:

> Opinions vary as to whether illegal aliens are a net cost or a net benefit to the United States. At one extreme, a study done for the

Table 6

Tax Payments and Use of Public Programs by Illegal Aliens

Program Activity	Percentage of Respondent Participation
Input	
Social security taxes withheld	77.3
Federal income taxes withheld	73.2
Hospitalization payments withheld	44.0
Filed U.S. income tax returns	31.5
Output	
Used hospitals or clinics	27.4
Collected one or more weeks of unemployment insurance	3.9
Have children in U.S. schools	3.7
Participated in U.S.-funded job-training programs	1.4
Secured food stamps	1.3
Secured welfare payments	0.5

Source: North and Houstoun, "The Characteristics and Role of Illegal Aliens," p. 142.

INS in 1975 by ICF, Incorporated, estimated that consumption of social services by illegal aliens costs the taxpayer a net of more than $13 billion a year. At the other extreme, some studies, the North report and the San Diego County study for example, have concluded that they contribute more to our welfare system than they take out. . . .

Illegal aliens do pay taxes—Federal and State income taxes, Social Security taxes, sales tax, gasoline tax, and property taxes—but how much is uncertain. In four major studies, interviews of current and former illegal aliens indicated that while they were employed in the United States, 66 to 81 percent had paid Federal income and Social Security taxes in the form of withholding from wages. In our interviews, 71 percent of the 96 who had been employed in the United States said Federal income tax had been withheld and 74 percent said their employers had withheld Social Security tax. . . .

Studies have also shown, however, that illegal aliens evade or underpay taxes. An Internal Revenue Service (IRS) official told us that he had no doubt that this occurs but that there is no way to estimate the extent. He said that based on IRS studies, IRS believes it "represents a low level of fraud commensurate with the general lower wage levels involved" and has a very minimal tax impact.

The net impact of illegal aliens' tax contributions toward support of the welfare system cannot be estimated with available information.[34]

One of the reasons that illegal aliens are detected so infrequently in public assistance programs is simply that participation increases the risk of detection, which leads to deportation. Although North and Houstoun's data suggest that illegal aliens do not actively participate in tax-supported programs directly, they may cause an increased indirect use of public assistance programs. If illegal aliens displace U.S. citizens from the labor market, these workers, in turn, may well become recipients of public assistance. North and Houstoun argue: "We do not know, and cannot know the extent to which the illegals we interviewed caused other workers to draw unemployment insurance benefits, or to rely on food stamps or welfare. Given the inadequate data on these indirect impacts, those who have written on the subject have been forced to use a process of building assumptions upon assumptions."[35]

Other Impacts

The prime motivation for illegal aliens to enter the United States is the prospect of employment at higher wages than are available in the country of origin. It is therefore not surprising that illegal aliens send substantial sums to their native countries.

According to North and Houstoun, Mexican illegals send home the largest monthly remittances, on average. In particular, those apprehended in counties bordering Mexico made the largest average payments to homeland relatives even though their average weekly wage was by far the lowest. This finding is consistent with the conclusion of Smith and Newman that illegal aliens may remain in areas near the border because of their "cultural heritage" or a closer attachment to their homeland. Assuming that about a million Mexican illegals are working in the United States, North and Houstoun estimate that $1.5 billion is sent to Mexico annually by illegal aliens. These payments support, on the average, 5.4 persons compared with 3.6 dependents for other Western Hemisphere respondents and 1.8 for Eastern Hemisphere illegals.[36]

Although it is impossible to determine the total amount sent abroad each year by illegal aliens, it appears that at least several billion dollars are involved. These funds have implications for U.S. international economic policy because the remittances sent abroad worsen the already unfavorable balance of payments of the United States. On the other side of this issue, this money can be regarded as a form of foreign aid, and a sudden halt to these payments or even a significant reduction could have undesirable consequences, particularly for Mexico. As an example, *Business Week* reports:

> State Department officials warn that for some of the most important countries of origin, such as Mexico, the shock of simultaneously losing the money that most aliens send home and of also having to reintegrate them into their slow-growing economies would be sure to worsen diplomatic relations with the U.S. and might heighten their social and political instability. Furthermore, many private organizations, most notably the Catholic Church and interested ethnic groups such as the Chicano "la Raza," argue vigorously that such a massive upheaval would be repugnant on humanitarian grounds.[37]

Proponents of more rigid enforcement of the immigration laws cite the 1975 Annual Report of the Immigration and Naturalization Service as proof that illegal aliens contribute heavily to the crime and drug problem in the United States. This report (pp. 12-21) shows that the INS seized 134 tons of marijuana and 3,659 ounces of hard drugs. Opponents of more rigid enforcement argue that it is conjectural whether such traffic in drugs would cease if the number of illegal aliens seeking employment were reduced. They point out that, as a group, illegal aliens are typically law-abiding individuals—of more than 766,000 deportable aliens located in 1975, only 202 were armed at the time of arrest. It is readily apparent that one of the least desirable events for an illegal alien is an encounter with legal authorities.

The long-term question of assimilation has also generated a certain amount of concern. Those opposed to increased alien immigration point to the problem the French-speaking population of Quebec is causing in English-speaking Canada. These opponents see the existence of a large Cuban population in Miami and of Spanish-speaking people in certain areas of the Southwest as pointing toward a potential Balkanization of American society. This view is not, however, uniformly shared. The counterargument has been offered that the United States has historically been a haven for immigrants and is in fact a nation of immigrants.

PENDING LEGISLATION

Three bills currently before the U.S. Congress pertain to the control of illegal aliens. Two represent the administration's position: H.R. 9531 was introduced by Representative Peter W. Rodino, Jr. (D-N.J.) on October 12, 1977; S. 2252 was introduced by Senators James O. Eastland (D-Miss.), Edward M. Kennedy (D-Mass.), Lloyd M. Bentsen (D-Tex.), and Dennis DeConcini (D-Ariz.) on October 28, 1977. An additional bill, S. 993 was introduced by Senator Robert Packwood (R-Ore.) on March 14, 1977. Although all three bills seek to amend the Immigration and Nationality Act, they are rather different in their legislative purposes: H.R. 9531 and S. 2252 concentrate on amnesty and the adjustment of alien status, whereas the express purpose of S. 993 is to achieve the "location and removal from employment . . . [of] those persons illegally employed and to check future employees prior to employment so as to ascertain their legal right thereto." The only provision common to all three bills is the hiring restriction imposed on employers, as discussed below.

Administration Bills (H.R. 9531 and S. 2252)

The major provisions of the administration bills are as follows:

Amnesty. H.R. 9531 and S. 2252 would authorize the attorney general, at his discretion, to create a record of lawful admission for permanent residence in the case of aliens who entered the United States prior to January 1, 1970, and who have been continuously in residence since entry. For inclusion in this category, aliens must also show the attorney general that they are not inadmissible under the section of the Immigration and Nationality Act barring criminals, procurers, and other immoral persons, subversives, violators of the narcotics laws, or smugglers of aliens. In addition, to be accepted under this heading, an alien must not have discriminated against any person because of race, religion, nationality, membership in a particular social group, or political opinion.

Numerical Entry Restrictions. With certain exceptions—special immigrants, immediate relatives of U.S. citizens, and resident illegal aliens covered by the amnesty provisions of the act—no more than 170,000 aliens from the Eastern Hemisphere could be issued visas for entry into the United States each year. The equivalent limit for the Western Hemisphere would be 120,000 immigrants per year.

21

Adjustment of Alien Status. The act would permit any illegal alien in the United States to continue to reside in this country for five years from the effective date of the administration bills, but only if application for this status is made within one year of enactment. To be eligible for this section, an alien would have to satisfy the attorney general that entry into the United States occurred before January 1, 1977, and that residence in the United States has been continuous since such entry. In addition, aliens would have to prove they were not inadmissable under the section of the Immigration and Nationality Act, discussed above, dealing with criminal activities or under that section dealing with discrimination. The adjustment of alien status provided by this section would not be available to aliens who were classified as: a non-immigrant on authorized stay in the United States on January 1, 1977; a non-immigrant student prior to losing lawful nonimmigrant status; or a nonimmigrant exchange alien under a two-year foreign residence requirement. To implement this section, the attorney general would have the power to authorize: documentation of alien status under this provision; employment under the alien status granted in this provision; readmission "of any alien who has temporary resident alien status . . . who is returning to a residence in the United States from a temporary visit abroad, without requiring such alien to obtain a passport, immigrant visa, reentry permit or other documentation"; and rescission of temporary resident alien status if it appears that an alien was not eligible for such status. Finally, no alien granted temporary resident status would be eligible for medical assistance under Title XIX of the Social Security Act, aid to families with dependent children (AFDC) under Title IV, part A, of the Social Security Act, aged blind or disabled benefits under Title XVI of the Social Security Act, or food stamps under the Food Stamp Act of 1964.

Restrictions on Employment of Aliens. The administration bills would make it unlawful for an employer to hire illegal aliens unless the employment were authorized by the attorney general. Violations of this provision would subject the employer to a civil penalty of not more than $1,000 for each illegal alien so employed. Proof that the employer saw documentary evidence that the illegal alien was eligible to work in the United States would raise a rebuttable presumption that the employer has not violated this section with respect to that particular person.

Procuring Employment for Illegal Aliens. The administration bills would make it a felony for any person knowingly and for gain to assist an illegal alien in obtaining or keeping employment in the United States. Conviction for such an offense would carry a fine of up to $2,000 or five years' imprisonment or both for each illegal alien who is the subject of a violation.

State and Local Preemption. If enacted, the administration bills would preempt any state or local laws imposing civil or criminal penalties on those who employ or facilitate the employment of illegal aliens.

Packwood Bill

The Packwood bill, while pursuing the same general objectives as the administration bills, approaches the illegal alien problem in a slightly different manner. A significant difference in this bill is that those who employ illegal aliens, along with those who serve as brokers or contract for their employment, would be guilty of a criminal misdemeanor punishable by a fine of up to $1,000 for each alien involved. Subsequent offenses would carry the same penalty. In addition, the Packwood bill includes provisions for monitoring the status of aliens and for making exceptions to the rules governing entry.

Monitoring of Alien Status. The Social Security Administration would be required to issue social security numbers only to U.S. citizens, aliens lawfully admitted to the United States for permanent residence, and other aliens under separate authority of law. Social security cards held by aliens not admitted for permanent residence would have to state plainly that the holder was not eligible for employment. The Social Security Administration would be required to examine all records to determine whether any individual is identified by a social security number and whether the number was properly issued. The Small Business Administration would be required to conduct employer surveys to determine whether employees have shown their employers a social security card and two items of supporting identification.

Exemptions for Employment. The Packwood bill provides that if a governor certifies the existence of an agricultural labor shortage in his state, the attorney general would be required to permit the temporary admission of nonimmigrant aliens to eliminate that shortage. The attorney general may require employers of aliens to pay a fee to cover the administration costs of the program or to post a bond to insure the departure of nonimmigrant aliens, either to the next employer or from the United States.

DISCUSSION OF THE ISSUES

A number of proposals in the various bills dealing with illegal aliens are currently subject to debate. The following is a brief survey of the arguments that have been made both for and against these proposals.

Employer Penalties

Advocates of employer penalties argue that the primary reason for the illegal alien problem is the availability of employment opportunities for nonimmigrant aliens in the United States. Aliens violate the law to seek employment because they know jobs can be found.[38]

> Based on all available information, U.S. employees are willing to hire illegal aliens in spite of, and sometimes because of, their illegal status. Illegal aliens are frequently willing to work for lower wages than U.S. workers because of the lower standards of living to which they are accustomed. They are also susceptible to exploitation in the form of substandard wages, working conditions, and minimal fringe benefits because of their fear of being reported to Immigration and Naturalization Service authorities.[39]

In other words, employers in the United States are willing to hire illegal aliens because of economic incentives and the fact that it is not illegal. As President Carter has stated: "The principal attraction of the United States for undocumented aliens is economic—the opportunity to obtain a job paying considerably more than any available in their own countries. If that opportunity is severely restricted, I am convinced that far fewer aliens will attempt illegal entry."[40]

INS Commissioner Leonard Chapman, writing in the October 1976 issue of *Reader's Digest,* argued that legislation was desperately needed to make employers shoulder a greater responsibility for enforcement. Proponents agree that employer penalties would supply a deterrent to hiring illegal aliens that does not now exist. They argue that enforcement would not be costly since there would be a high level of voluntary compliance, and those employers choosing to violate the law would, in large part, be known to INS.[41]

Opponents of employer penalties generally do not argue directly against the efficacy of the proposed sanctions. Their three basic lines of arguments are based on other grounds that they feel justify forgoing this method of preventing the employment of illegal aliens.

First, employers argue that it is difficult to determine whether an employee or prospective employee is an illegal alien or not, and in any event it is the job of the INS to patrol the borders and monitor alien status so that illegal aliens are kept out of the U.S. labor markets.[42] Employers argue that holding them liable for hiring illegal aliens improperly makes them responsible for law enforcement. This difficulty is compounded by the fact that many illegal aliens pose as U.S. citizens and have forged identification to support their claims.

In an interconnected argument, civil rights groups see the imposition of employer penalties as leading to discrimination against ethnic minorities.[43] This would occur if employers, faced with penalties for hiring illegal aliens, request documentary proof of citizenship or legal residence only from obvious members of ethnic minorities. Another response by employers could be a refusal to hire members of an ethnic minority because of a subjective assessment that their appearance alone suggests an illegal status.

A final objection to the imposition of employer penalties concerns the cost of this type of program.[44] Opponents argue that the federal cost of checking on employers would be immense, and the costs to employers, while unknown, would surely be of sufficient magnitude to justify eliminating the employer penalty provisions.

Amnesty

Advocates of amnesty for illegal aliens, including the Carter administration, argue that its primary purpose is to reduce the exploitation of aliens and the depressing effects they exert on wages and working conditions. An additional argument offered in favor of amnesty concerns the large number of illegal aliens who have accumulated considerable equity in this country, not to mention the close family ties that have likely been developed.[45]

Some economists have defended amnesty entirely on economic grounds. They contend that the shortage of legal, secondary, unskilled workers created a demand in this country for illegal alien labor and that the level of unemployment and welfare benefits is a primary cause of this shortage. Migrant workers from the rural south and Puerto Rico formerly held these jobs, but these labor sources were exhausted by the mid-1960s. Now manufacturing industries such as shoes and textiles, service industries such as restaurants and hospitals, and other secondary employers have become dependent upon illegal alien labor. It is therefore argued that, before any stringent controls on illegals are initiated, a broad amnesty must be granted so that the pool of low-cost labor is not destroyed.[46]

President Carter explained further that amnesty for humanitarian reasons was a necessary part of his program to avoid having a permanent underclass of millions of persons who have not been and cannot practicably be deported, and who would continue living here in perpetual fear of immigration authorities, the local police, employers and neighbors. Their entire existence would continue to be predicated on staying outside the reach of government authorities and law's protection.[47]

Opponents of amnesty provisions for illegal aliens argue that this would simply legalize the theft of U.S. jobs by foreigners. In support of this argument, opponents point to the current level of unemployment in the U.S. and argue that this could be greatly reduced by removing illegal aliens and replacing them with now unemployed Americans or legally resident aliens eligible for employment. In addition, opponents argue that this amnesty provision, if enacted, would have an unexpected twofold effect: aliens would flood into the United States in an attempt to take advantage of the amnesty through the use of forged papers, and more aliens would enter in anticipation of future amnesties. This would make the job of controlling entry into the U.S. even more difficult than it is today. Opponents also argue that amnesty implicitly condones law breaking and gives an unfair advantage to illegal aliens over aliens who have attempted to comply with the law.[48]

Identity Cards

Another proposal is to issue a card to all residents of the United States showing their eligibility for employment. Advocates of this approach argue that it would not unduly burden employees but would prevent illegal aliens from taking U.S. jobs. They argue that with the issuance of identity cards to persons legally entitled to work, problems of identification and discrimination would virtually disappear. To the charge that a national identity card constitutes an intolerable infringement on civil liberties, advocates have replied that:

> What is un-American is the invasion of privacy. The documentation of individual Americans is not in itself a violation of privacy. What is done with that documentation is what matters. . . . Before the age of passports, there were no passport numbers; but there is no rational resentment of passports nowadays, if it is conceded that the identification of the individual is important. . . . An identity card is not the solution, it is merely one device to aid in the regulation of one problem. The presumptive philosophical objections to it ought to be analyzed. If we believe that a country has the right to regulate citizenship by a rhythm suitable to its own priorities, then it follows that a country has the right to seek the means of distinguishing between those people within its frontiers who are citizens, and those who are not.[49]

Proponents of the identity card regard the social security card as potentially serving the identity function. It is believed that only minor changes would be necessary to convert this card into legal evidence of the right to work.[50]

Opposition to an identity card program is generally based on two arguments. The first is posed by civil libertarians who believe that a work permit monitored by the central government would constitute a serious threat to individual liberty.[51] They view this threat as self-evident whenever the government moves to control or gather information on the lives of individual private citizens.

The Social Security Administration itself opposes the use of its cards as proof of legal status. Its first objection is based on the immense cost of creating and distributing a new card that would be immune to forgery or alteration. The second argument is that tying this additional purpose to the social security card would ultimately degrade a system originally intended to coordinate potential benefit rights with earnings.[52] The level of truthful, voluntary compliance with social security requirements could be expected to decline as the "stakes" in the right to work increased in value.

ALTERNATIVE PROPOSALS

Temporary Alien Workers

Since it is virtually impossible to stop the flow of illegal aliens so long as the U.S. income level diverges drastically from that in the alien's country of origin, it is suggested that a practical solution would be to allow controlled entry of temporary alien workers. In this way nonimmigrant aliens could be legally channeled to areas where labor shortages exist. If this prescription were followed, there would be no direct competition for U.S. jobs, and giving legal status to alien labor would effectively discourage exploitation.[53]

Opponents of a controlled entry program argue that unemployment rates in the United States are already extremely high among groups that would be likely to compete with nonimmigrant aliens.[54] They call for programs to increase the mobility of secondary workers in the United States rather than an expansion of alien worker traffic.

Redesigning U.S. Immigration Policy

A recent survey of illegal aliens found that a large number of those interviewed held jobs for which labor certification would have been automatically rejected if they had attempted to enter the country legally.[55] It is argued that the liberalization of numerical and occupational restrictions on immigration would increase the opportunities for legal entry and reduce the demand for illegal entrants.

Opponents argue that loosening legal entry requirements would simply increase the number of legal aliens and have no effect on the flow of illegal aliens. They contend that the final result of a liberalized immigration policy would be more competition for U.S. jobs that are already in short supply.

Adequacy of Resources for Dealing with Illegal Aliens

It has been argued that the Immigration and Naturalization Service is grossly understaffed and underfinanced. Although 1,700 of the U.S. Border Patrol's 2,000 officers are located along the Mexican-U.S. border where the vast majority of the illegal aliens enter the United States, there is only one patrolman for every ten miles of border.[56] Concentrated inspection efforts at selected ports of entry yielded a rejection of alien entrants at a rate twelve to fourteen times greater than the rate during routine operations.[57] Proponents argue that increased expenditures to enforce existing legislation would ultimately be less costly than many new proposals and would cause less social damage. In addition, greater investment in resources for the Border Patrol and visa inspection would stop illegal entry at the source and would eliminate not only the domestic economic problem created by alien infiltration but also the more costly internal search for illegal aliens.[58]

Opposition to increased funding for the enforcement of current legislation centers around the argument that as long as job opportunities for illegal aliens are available in this country, it is impossible for the INS and the State Department to restrict entry effectively. Many oppose additional spending for enforcement on the ground that economy in government is a more important issue.[59]

Strict Enforcement of Related Legislation

Many people argue that new legislation is not needed to penalize employers of illegal aliens because existing laws would accomplish the same purpose if enforced. Under existing tax and labor laws all laborers are supposed to receive the minimum wage, and employers must deduct social security and income taxes from the payrolls of aliens as well as citizen workers. If these laws were strictly enforced the competitive advantage of illegal aliens would be reduced. In addition, employers could be cited for violating occupational safety and health regulations in many instances where substandard work conditions are used to exploit illegal aliens.[60]

Arguments against this approach claim that it would be impossible to achieve the degree of coordination among government agencies necessary for the strict enforcement of legislation related to the illegal alien problem. Most agencies believe that it is the responsibility of INS to deal with illegal aliens and consequently do not feel any special obligation to operate in this area.[61]

NOTES TO TEXT

[1] Leonard F. Chapman, Jr., "Illegal Aliens: Time to Call a Halt," *Reader's Digest*, October 1976, p. 191.

[2] Elliott Abrams and Franklin S. Abrams, "Immigration Policy—Who Gets In and Why?" *The Public Interest*, vol. 38 (Winter 1975), pp. 21-22.

[3] Act of October 19, 1888, 25 Stat. 566.

[4] Act of February 5, 1917, 39 Stat. 874.

[5] Act of May 26, 1924, 43 Stat. 153.

[6] Act of June 27, 1952, Public Law 82-414, 66 Stat. 163, 8 U.S.C. 1011 ff.

[7] Act of October 3, 1965, Public Law 89-236, 79 Stat. 911.

[8] Act of October 20, 1976, Public Law 94-571, 90 Stat. 2703.

[9] Act of December 7, 1974, Public Law 93-518, 88 Stat. 1652.

[10] Act of October 30, 1972, Public Law 92-603, 86 Stat. 1329.

[11] Act of October 20, 1976, Public Law 94-566, 90 Stat. 2680.

[12] David S. North and Marion S. Houstoun, "The Characteristics and Role of Illegal Aliens in the U.S. Labor Market: An Exploratory Study" (Washington, D.C.: Linton & Co., March 1976). This report was prepared for the Employment and Training Administration of the U.S. Department of Labor.

[13] Ibid., pp. S-1 ff. By selecting aliens of at least sixteen years of age who had worked for wages for at least two weeks in the United States, North and Houstoun concentrated on an important subset of illegal aliens, namely those in the labor market. These aliens are distinctly atypical, however, because the Immigration and Naturalization Service reports that 57 percent of the illegal aliens caught are apprehended within seventy-two hours of entry. See U.S. Department of Justice, Immigration and Naturalization Service, *1975 Annual Report*, p. 13.

[14] North and Houstoun, "The Characteristics and Role of Illegal Aliens," p. 107.

[15] Ibid., p. 36.

[16] "What Illegal Aliens Cost the Economy," *Business Week*, June 13, 1977.

[17] Barton Smith and Robert Newman, "Depressed Wages along the U.S.-Mexico Border: An Empirical Analysis," *Economic Inquiry*, vol. 15 (January 1977), pp. 62-63.

[18] Ibid., p. 53.

[19] Ibid., p. 63.

[20] "Border Crisis: Illegal Aliens Out of Control?" *U.S. News and World Report*, April 25, 1977.

[21] "What Illegal Aliens Cost the Economy," *Business Week*, June 13, 1977.

[22] "A Doubly Difficult Apple to Pluck," *Time*, November 7, 1977.

[23] Michael J. Piore, "Impact of Immigration on the Labor Force," *Monthly Labor Review*, vol. 98 (May 1975), pp. 41-43.

[24] U.S. Congress, House, Committee on the Judiciary, *Illegal Aliens: Analysis and Background*, 1977, p. 52.

[25] Phillip Cagan, "The Reduction of Inflation and the Magnitude of Unemployment," in William Fellner, ed., *Contemporary Economic Problems 1977* (Washington, D.C.: American Enterprise Institute, 1977), pp. 27 and 28 ff.

[26] See U.S. Congress, House, *Illegal Aliens: Analysis and Background*, p. 21.

[27] Comptroller General of the United States, *Impact of Illegal Aliens on Public Assistance Programs: Too Little Is Known*, Report to the Senate Committee on the Budget, December 1, 1977, p. 3; hereafter cited as GAO report.

[28] Ibid., pp. 2-3.

[29] Ibid., pp. 15-16.

[30] Chapman, "Illegal Aliens: Time to Call a Halt," p. 188.

[31] GAO report, p. 14.

[32] North and Houstoun, "The Characteristics and Role of Illegal Aliens," p. 98.

[33] Ibid., p. 149.

[34] GAO report, p. 14.

[35] North and Houstoun, "The Characteristics and Role of Illegal Aliens," p. 140.

[36] Ibid., pp. 78-81.

[37] "What Illegal Aliens Cost the Economy," *Business Week*, June 13, 1977.

[38] U.S. Congress, House, Committee on the Judiciary, *Amending the Immigration and Nationality Act, and for Other Purposes*, Report of the Committee to Accompany H.R. 8713, September 24, 1975, House Report 94-506, p. 6.

[39] Joyce Vialet, *Illegal Aliens*, Issue Brief no. IB74137 (Washington, D.C.: Library of Congress Research Service, Major Issues System, November 1974; updated February 1978).

[40] Executive Office of the President, *Undocumented Aliens*, 95th Cong., 1st sess., August 4, 1977, House Doc. no. 95-202, p. 2.

[41] U.S. Domestic Council Committee on Illegal Aliens, *Preliminary Report*, December 1976, p. 241.

[42] David S. North and Marion S. Houstoun, "A Summary of Recent Data on and Some of the Public Policy Implications of Illegal Immigration," in *Illegal Aliens: An Assessment of the Issues* (Washington, D.C.: National Council on Employment Policy, October 1976), p. 178.

[43] Ibid.

[44] U.S. Congress, House, *Illegal Aliens: Analysis and Background*, p. 57.

[45] Ibid., p. 59.

[46] Michael J. Piore, "Illegal Immigration in the United States: Some Observations and Policy Suggestions," in *Illegal Aliens: An Assessment of Issues*, pp. 28-35.

[47] Executive Office of the President, *Undocumented Aliens*, p. 4.

[48] U.S. Congress, House, *Illegal Aliens: Analysis and Background*, p. 60.

[49] William F. Buckley, "In Defense of Identity Cards," *Washington Star*, November 1, 1977; reprinted in the *Congressional Record*, December 8, 1977, p. S19465.

[50] National Council on Employment Policy, "Public Policy toward Alien Workers," in *Illegal Aliens: An Assessment of the Issues*, p. 3.

[51] U.S. Domestic Council Committee on Illegal Aliens, *Preliminary Report*, p. 179.

[52] Ibid., p. 95.

[53] Alejandro Portes, "Return of the Wetback," *Society,* vol. 11 (March/April 1974), p. 46.

[54] U.S. Congress, House, *Illegal Aliens: Analysis and Background*, p. 62.

[55] North and Houstoun, "Summary of Recent Data," p. 111.

[56] U.S. Domestic Council Committee on Illegal Aliens, *Preliminary Report*, p. 84.

[57] U.S. Department of Justice, Immigration and Naturalization Service, *Illegal Alien Study*, Pt. 1, *Fraudulent Entrants Study*, September 1976.

[58] U.S. Domestic Council Committee on Illegal Aliens, *Preliminary Report*, p. 123.

[59] U.S. Congress, House, *Illegal Aliens: Analysis and Background*, p. 66.

[60] North and Houstoun, "Summary of Recent Data," p. 47.

[61] U.S. Domestic Council Committee on Illegal Aliens, *Preliminary Report*, p. 241.

DATE DUE

DE 7'93			
JA 4'94			
NO 30 0			
MY 06 0			
AP 2 1 4			